Less Than

A story of triumph

By Jennifer Munson

This book is dedicated to the two loves of my life, my amazing sons, Dante & Isaiah. You will never truly know the depths of my love for you and how your lives had a hand in saving mine. I pray you love the Lord our God with all your hearts, souls, and minds all the days of your lives.

INTRODUCTION

This is my story. Not my mother's, father's, sister's, brother's, nor my son's. May God be glorified in all that I write. The purpose of this book is to share of God's goodness, mercy, grace, and love in hopes that others may come to the cross, or come back to the cross, and take part in all that it offers.

As I write this today I am now a strong woman of God who knows what it's like to live in the goodness of the Lord. He has brought me so very far and there is nothing that would every take me back to the bondage of sin again. I no longer feel less than anyone else, I know that God has chosen me for something special. I work for a large ministry and have the opportunity to write for thousands of readers. I am a true testament of what God can do through a yielded vessel. He truly makes beauty out of ashes.

Writing this book has been a painful process. Many things I had forgotten until I started writing. I've shed a lot of tears as I wrote, realizing how much pain I went through and how many times God was protecting me when I thought He wasn't even there. I've learned that once the pain has been revealed, the healing process begins. So I invite you to take this journey with me and experience the healing power of God. Read how God took me from a girl who felt less than her entire life to a powerful woman of God that many come to for guidance.

CHAPTER 1

I have many memories from my childhood, and life did not start out easy. However, the many things I have endured have shaped who I am today. It is incredible the way God protected and provided for my family. I pray as you read my story that you see only God's goodness.

My parents married young, my mom just seventeen and my father, twenty-three. We were poor and even lived in a tent for a short time in my father's parents yard. I was less than two at the time, so I really don't remember much about it. I imagine it was difficult for my parents to provide for us during this time. My mom did not work, as my father did not allow it, even though my father found it difficult to hold down a steady job.

I loved spending time with my grandmother, my mom's mother, as I grew up. She called me her princess (I was the first granddaughter), and she would brush my hair, put curlers in, teach me how to fold laundry and iron clothes. I always felt special when I was with her. My other grandmother was similar, but I didn't spend as much time with her. She taught me how to sew and took me to the store and let me choose things to buy.

When I was still a toddler, we started going to church and my parents found the Lord and accepted Christ as their Savior. This gave me a lot of hope and strength as we endured hardships. We often did not have much money for even the essentials like heat, hot water, and food. It was normal living for us. Wearing your coat to stay warm in the house was a common occurrence and I never thought differently about it. I remember at times coming home to a box of food on our porch, or a check slipped under the door. My mom did an amazing job of protecting us from the hardship. She never made it seem like we were lacking anything or that we should feel sorry for ourselves.

We never stayed in one house for too long, moving to a new place every few years, but there's one house where I have the most memories. It was and old farmhouse in a town called Honeybrook, in Pennsylvania just outside Philadelphia and just close enough to Amish Country to see horses and buggies as we drove. We were surrounded by corn fields, which I loved to play in, especially since there weren't any neighbors close by. My brother and I would spend hours in the fields playing "Hide and Go Seek", making forts, and other fun activities.

At a young age, I felt the need to earn approval from my parents. Their love and attention seemed difficult for me to achieve. I tried to do everything right without being asked. I was mature even at a young age, always trying to earn my parents love and attention. I helped with chores, took care of my younger sisters, and tried my best to not get in trouble. I even won first place in the art contest in first grade. The better my behavior however, the less my parents needed to parent me and consequently the less they would parent me. This made me feel even more unworthy.

That feeling continued as I grew. I remember seeing my father holding my sister on his lap and wondering why he didn't do that with me. I didn't understand why he didn't love me like he loved my sisters.

My parents were not very affectionate with me and "I love you" wasn't something that was just thrown freely around. What I would have given to hear those words. I thought I needed to find a way to be better, or do more, to earn my parents love. My aunts and grandmother told me that as a child, I wouldn't let them hug me or hold me, because I did not like to be touched. My mom said I was always mature, always responsible. I can even see it when I look back at pictures of when I was young, and how I carried myself, what I thought of myself. I remember always feeling like an outsider, at home or at school. Always less than everyone else.

I always had a sense of unworthiness I carried, which was mistaken for shyness or being quiet. The Bible says, "The tongue has the power of life and death, and those who love it will eat its fruit," (Proverbs 18:21 NIV). I always heard "Jennifer is shy." Hearing those words as a child convinced me that I was shy, and I lived that belief. So even if I was outgoing, I heard "she is shy" so many times that I believed it, and it created a root from which grew many things. I wasn't just shy, I felt worthless. I thought I didn't matter. I thought I wasn't good enough, or pretty enough. I had no confidence, because the devil was busy whispering lies that no one loved me. I constantly felt less than.

The devil took words spoken by my parents and twisted them into lies. I have read that when a woman is pregnant and constantly says she doesn't want the baby, that rejection can be felt even while the baby is still in the womb. In the Bible, we read that our words have power. Psalm 45:1 "... my tongue is the pen of a skillful writer." Stories are written with the tongue; and we need to be aware of what story we are creating for children around us. My story from the beginning was one of feeling less than everyone else.

CHAPTER 2

As I grew older, the devil continually whispered in my ear, telling me lies, but I did not realize that then, I believed every word. He told me my parents didn't love me that I wasn't as important as the other children, and what I did mattered little. Because of those lies, I decided to create my own reality. I loved to daydream and make up scenarios of how my life could be. I day dreamed of owning a horse and having my own farm, or being with friends wearing a pretty dress, and sometimes pretended I had a boyfriend. I continued to make up scenarios that were not real throughout my entire life. The more I daydreamed, the more I heard ideas in my head. For this reason I liked to be alone, then I could create whatever reality I wanted, where I was safe, I was important, and I mattered. I was able to create another me who was appreciated, wanted, and loved. I imagined being happy with friends. I dreamed of walking with Jesus in heaven. I also imagined having a boyfriend and the things he would say to me, such as how much he liked me. I imagined living in a nicer place. As I grew older, the daydreams changed.

I loved reading because it helped my imagination and gave me ideas and scenarios to put myself in. Most of the books I read were from Scholastic, and they were all innocent books. *Are you there God? It's me, Margaret*, and other Judy Blume books. They took my mind off how I felt about myself and let me dream of a different life.

Being alone was a way that the devil isolated me, so that the lies stayed alive in my mind and I was continually creating a false sense of reality.

I disliked how I felt in real life so I would escape to my own world. As I got older, I told men I dated that I was very independent and didn't need others and that is why I was ok with being alone. This was another lie I believed from Satan. I learned later that when I was alone, I became vulnerable to attack. The comfort I felt from being by myself came from hearing the lies so often year after year, they were my normal and I felt comfort from them. To clarify, I've heard those lies as voices in my head for thirty-eight years. I did not realize they were not supposed to be there, all of those years, I thought it was an inner voice.

CHAPTER 3

When I was in elementary school, my father started working for Bible Baptist Church and West Chester Christian School as a shop teacher and also handled the sound for church services. Because he worked there, we were able to attend the Christian school.

At the age of six, I prayed and asked Jesus to come into my heart and save me. I had a strong desire to share God with others. Missionary work became my passion when I asked Jesus into my heart. My mom wrote in her journal, "Jennifer asked me to lead her to the Lord! I showed her some verses and we prayed. She cried and said she was afraid. She also said she wanted to be a missionary. She told me she *was* a lost sheep." I know that God gave me a missionary's heart and it's easy to see that I felt that calling even at the age of six. Each time I heard missionaries come to speak about the work they did, and the peoples' lives they touched my heart longed to be a part of it. I had visions of being in a faraway country surrounded by children that needed to know about God.

When I was in the first grade, I got sick. At first they thought I had the stomach flu, but when I did not get better, the doctors eventually realized my appendix had burst. Usually when that happens, sepsis occurs, which is when the bacteria inside the appendix spreads through your bloodstream like poison and causes death. But miraculously, something blocked it from spreading through my body. God was with me. I remember my pastor coming and praying with me, and all the cards my first grade class made wishing me well.

During my hospital stay, I had an angel visit me. I had never spent the night away from home and my mom was extremely worried about me. I had a roommate, but after she was discharged, the angel stayed with me. Everything about him was gentle, kind, and peaceful. He had dark long hair, but not quite to his shoulders. He was tall, thin, and was always smiling. He sat next to my bed and played the lyre and we sang about Jesus all night. I remember him like it was yesterday. I look back now and think maybe the devil was trying to take my life, maybe because of my love for Jesus, or maybe because he could've guessed what I might do for the Kingdom of God as I got older. But God's plans for me could not be destroyed. In Job, it says, "I know that you can do all things no plan of yours can be thwarted" (Job 42:2 NIV).

My mom came to the hospital the next morning and when she got to my room she asked how my night by myself was, and I told her, "Great! A man stayed with me."

As you can imagine, she became very upset, and ran out to the nurse's desk, where they told her that no one went into my room at all. I remember she asked me to draw a picture of the instrument he played. As I did, she realized it was an instrument from Bible times, and that the "man" was actually an angel. Angels are mentioned many times in the Bible appearing to people in both the Old and New Testament. Hebrews 1:14 says, "Are not all angels ministering spirits sent to serve those who will inherit salvation?" Another favorite verse tells us to be careful how we treat strangers, because it might be an angel. "Do not forget to show hospitality to strangers for by so doing some people have shown hospitality to angels without knowing it" (Hebrews 13:2 NIV). God sends his angels to protect us, "For He shall give His angels charge over you, to keep you in all your ways" (Psalm 91:11 NKJV). What a special encounter, one that has stayed closed to my heart throughout the years.

After I was discharged from the hospital, I remember having special time with my mom during my time of recovery at home. We didn't do anything out of the ordinary, but I had her all to myself, and it made me so happy, I finally felt special instead of less than. I don't remember feeling that way often.

CHAPTER 4

We had a service at school with special speakers and I felt God tugging at my heart and I was excited to see what God would do in my life. At the age of eleven, I dedicated my life to full-time service. A couple of women from the church would take me to the Pocopson Nursing Home to pray and sing with the elderly. I would go into the rooms and sometimes just sit and hold their hands as they talked. Other times I would sing as they sat and listened. Their faces would light up, and I felt loved, as if what I was doing mattered. I also loved the attention. I enjoyed sharing God's love and joy with others; it gave me a sense of worthiness I didn't feel otherwise.

Growing up, restrictions were given to us including not watching much TV, listening to the radio, going to the movies, dancing, and interaction with anyone outside of the church or school. I remember my father yelling at my mom and sometimes throwing and breaking things but my Mom protected us, so I didn't think too much about it.

I remember craving my father's approval, wanting him to notice me. I tried to be interested in the things he was interested in; drawing, skydiving, guns, motorcycles, selling Christmas trees, karate, it didn't matter what it was, I just wanted to be visible to him. I didn't realize that each hobby was something that took his time away from his family and a distraction that used money we didn't have to spend. Distractions are what they should have been called, not hobbies. I never felt he noticed me and that left a void, which ended up being filled with lies from Satan.

I want to point something out here. My brother and sisters could have been in the exact same situation, treated the exact same way, but because I had these lies in my mind and they were familiar to me, I felt completely different. Siblings can grow up in the same environment and have completely different feelings with completely different views of what happened. Satan got ahold of my mind at a very young age and my view of everything became shaded. It's like I had shades on that dimmed everything in the world, dimmed what was loving and pure.

We attended Sunday school, Sunday morning service, Sunday night service, Wednesday night Bible study, Thursday night evangelism and anything else that was going on at the church. We breathed and ate church and I loved it!

It was all I knew. We were taught that women were not to wear pants in church and were not allowed to be leaders in the church. I remember feeling sorry for the women who visited our church wearing pants because I knew for sure they were going to hell. I also felt sorry for the kids whose parents let them watch sitcoms, because I knew they were sinning. I thought anyone who didn't believe what I did or look like we did was going to hell. I've since learned we are not bound by law, but free by His unmerited favor. (Praise God!)

When I was in sixth grade, my parents sat my siblings and I down one day and told us we had a half-sister. I had no idea what they were talking about or what that meant. My father explained he had been married before and had a daughter. My sisters were too young to really understand what was going and I don't remember how my brother felt at that time, but I was excited and a little nervous.

She came over to our house and I was ecstatic about having a big sister. She wore makeup, had a car, and was so pretty! She started coming over regularly to spend time with my father, and it seemed he really enjoyed her being around. He bought her nice presents and I wondered why she was so special, and why she got things we didn't. Why was my father buying things for her that he never bought for my mom? My mom and half-sister got along, but it was obvious my "new" sister was special to my father. This was just one more person he loved more than me, one more person who was prettier and better than I was, and one more person who deserved the love I didn't.

I was about fifteen when one night I was sewing my culottes (no, I am not kidding and if you don't know what they are, google it.) for gym class the next day. It was late, and I overheard my mom and father talking downstairs. I heard my father say, "These kids are the only thing keeping this marriage together."

I was in shock; we were a perfect church family! I woke my brother up and told him what I had just heard, but he didn't believe me. He told me to go to bed, that I was wrong and confused. What we didn't realize as children is that our mom had hid so much from us. My father would yell at my mom, throw things and sometimes he just wouldn't come home. When he was at home he isolated himself. Not being very present with his family. My mom did a good job of protecting us from the chaos that went on. I never remember her crying or taking anything out on us. She was a rock and our protector from all the things my father was putting her through.

Eventually my father left, and everything got blurry to me. I learned he left to go live with my half-sister's mom, his first wife. I had so much bitterness towards my half-sister because I felt she was the reason my family was falling apart. Now *she* had her parents back together for holidays and for when she would get married and have children. I lost that and blamed her. Very quickly we found out we couldn't go to the Christian school anymore. I remember people at church looking at me differently and not saying much of anything at all. I don't remember what was said, but I know I felt different and was treated like an outsider. Hardly anyone in our church had a broken family. I felt judged even if I wasn't being judged. I think some looked at us with pity and didn't know what to say, but as a teen I took that as I was now an outcast, rejected. I didn't fit in anymore.

My friend, whose parents were also separating, would go with me to youth group, but after they dropped us off, we would walk up the street to a reservoir and smoke cigarettes. We didn't fit in anymore and we didn't want people looking at us or judging us for our parent's mistakes. We were angry, bitter and rebellious. We had bad attitudes and tried to keep to ourselves as much as possible.

The father of lies was in my ear and the words grew louder and stronger. "God isn't real, look at how these people are treating you after everything you have been taught. Your family didn't want you, neither does church, neither does God. You aren't good enough, you are different." The Bible tells us that the devil is the father of lies, he never tells the truth. It's dangerous when we believe his lies. John 8:44 (KJV) says, "You are of *your* father the devil, and the desires of your father you want to do. He was a murderer from the beginning, and does not stand in the truth, because there is no truth in him. When he speaks a lie, he speaks from his own *resources,* for he is a liar and the father of it."

I was put into public school, and it was terrifying. I was in culture shock and people thought I was either a snob or prejudice. But I quickly learned to adapt to my surroundings along with being the product of a single-parent home. Compared to Christian school, public school was so big and full of different races. It was loud, fast, extremely easy, and once I experienced it, I started to call Christian school, prison. No one was telling me what to wear or how to talk in public school. I didn't have to fit into a certain box to be accepted.

My mom also adapted. She had to work full-time and take care of a household by herself, which she had never done. She had never even balanced a checkbook, as my father had controlled everything. She found the world and things of the world to distract her from the overwhelming responsibilities waiting at home, including two teenagers who were bitter, angry, confused, and lashing out. She loved to go out with her friends. I'm sure her new found freedom felt good after so many years of being controlled by my father.

My two younger sisters still needed to be cared for. I was 15 and did what I could, but sometimes didn't feel like helping. I got angry and bitter towards my mom for making me miss out on things a teenager would normally be doing. My friends would go to the local roller rink and hang out, have sleepovers and go to the movies. I couldn't always go because I had to stay home with my sisters so my mom could go out. I remember my friends calling me asking me to go and when she would say no because she had plans I remember yelling at her. I was not happy with either of my parents and had little respect for them. Some days my mom wouldn't come home and I didn't know where she was, leaving me to be responsible for my younger sisters.

I was just a teenager taking on the role of a single parent, a weight that a child should not have to bare. Since I was home alone most of with the time, not being shown affection, not having any one saying I love you, the unworthiness continued to build. The lies were constant in my ear. "Your mom only wants you home so you can take care of her kids so she can go out. She doesn't care anything about you, that's why she doesn't like to come home."

One time, a man called for her and he asked who I was, so I told him. He said my mom told him I was just the babysitter. The devil whispered, "Of course she told him that. She never wanted you and she's ashamed she even had you." In reality, she just didn't want him to know her age. Normally, that might be funny and not a big deal, but because I was used to hearing these lies, and they were so familiar to me, I always believed what these voices said. Lies always cover up truth.

I started to hate my mom, and I mean really hate her. I wanted her to be miserable like me. I was not a nice teenager. I had so much anger and bitterness for so many reasons, but I took it all out on the one closest to me, my mom. I was disrespectful and did not want to help her in any way. Being a single mom is very hard. I know for I've been one for 19 years, but back then I had no idea the weight a single mom must carry and I blamed her for everything.

CHAPTER 5

I got a job and worked as much as possible so I could get out of the house and not be forced to watch my sisters. I also wanted to have the freedom of buying my own food and clothes since they were both hard to come by otherwise. My mom would sometimes forget to pick me up from my job at Frank's Nursery and Crafts. I heard the continual lies of my unworthiness as I sat in the parking lot alone at night. The devil convinced me that she didn't love me, and didn't even notice I was gone, so of course she would forget to pick me up. I shouldn't be surprised. His whisper continued in my ear.

At school, I felt like I didn't belong most of the time. The whispers told me, "You aren't like them. They have gone to school together since they were young, and you are some poor Christian girl that doesn't know anything about their music or how they dress. No one will like you. It's better to just keep to yourself." I had friends, of course, but I kept my distance except for just a few. All my friends were already having sex and I hadn't even thought about it. Guys were never a huge interest of mine and I didn't care much about them. When I did date, the guys always had a girlfriend already. I heard the lie, "You aren't good enough to be their girlfriend, so you have to settle for being the girl on the side. Plus, you are too independent to commit to them anyway. You don't need them. This way is much better because you still have your freedom."

I became friends with people who didn't think anything of not having food at home or not being allowed to turn on the heat in the winter. I learned that if I surrounded myself with people in the same situation they wouldn't judge me for not having the same. I missed a lot of school, I was depressed, and wanted to quit. My mom told me I could, because she was sick of fighting with me, but my PE teacher talked me into completing school. I remember telling her that I was going to quit and she took me in her office and talked with me. I don't remember what she said, but she cared enough to reach out and that meant something to me.

In my senior year I started to hang out with drug dealers and their girlfriends. Drug dealers have power and respect because of what they do, they wouldn't have otherwise and I was attracted to that. I also hung around other kids who didn't have parents at home and had learned how to survive. Not live, but survive.

After I graduated high school, I dated a guy who was married. He sold drugs and was much older than me and I was infatuated with him. I knew he did cocaine but he treated me well. He didn't treat me like I was the other woman, but made me feel like I was number one, his first choice. He took me to his family's bar and we would drink and he would get high. I actually liked when he was high, because he treated me better and would spend more time with me. He would surprise me and bring me dinner and tell me how pretty I was and that he didn't really want to be with his wife anymore. He was even thoughtful and kind towards my family. We spent a lot of time together and I thought I was in love. It didn't take long before I got pregnant but I didn't even know it until I lost the baby. It was very early on, and I was naïve. I was at work and blood was running down my legs and I was very dizzy. I had no choice but to tell my mom. She wasn't surprised I had gotten pregnant since many of my friends were having babies. We went right to the doctor, who firmly told me about birth control options. The guy I had been dating had already moved on to the next girl, and I never even told him what happened. I was so brokenhearted and felt rejected once again.

I was continuing in survival mode by adapting to my surroundings. I sold drugs, sometimes carried a gun, saw people stabbed, and went with drug dealers into crack houses to collect money. I saw a lot of ugliness. But these people became like family to me. They gave me a sense of belonging that I didn't feel anywhere else. I stayed away from my house as long as possible and usually only went home late at night.

This life on the streets was normal for the people I hung out with, and the town I lived in. We spent most of our nights hanging on the streets or inside playing cards, waiting for the crack heads to knock on the door for their drugs. I remember my best friend at the time being stabbed in the back multiple times while a crowd of people stood around watching. We had gone to the local deli to get food and someone standing waiting for their food to be made, kept staring at my friend like he had an issue. My friend did not like it, and was already hot tempered, so it didn't take much for him to get into an argument. They were fighting in the deli and crashed against the glass display, breaking it. They got outside and continued to fight, until the man took a large piece of the glass and stabbed my friend with it multiple times. I was crying out to those around me to help him, but everyone just stood and watched. I was in so much shock, I could barely talk. I helped him walk across the street as he bled until the ambulance came. He was taken to the hospital where he got stitches and was sent home with instructions to rest and keep the wounds clean. That was New Year's Eve of 1994, what a way to start the year. The year I would be in my first abusive relationship.

CHAPTER 6

At the age of nineteen, I met a man, Darius*, who is my son's father. He had been out of jail less than a week when I met him. Darius was tall and thin with brown eyes and tan skin; I was instantly attracted to him. He was bold, arrogant and spoke his mind. Our first conversation was an argument. That should have been a red flag, except for the fact that those traits were much like my father's and something I was comfortable being around. I was so starved for attention and love from a man, I gave him my phone number and he called me in the middle of the night that same night.

The devil knows just when to put someone into our path, he isolates us, and tells us lies at just the right moment. He then[1] slips someone in who will help you continue in your destruction. He is always seeking to kill and destroy those who love God.

My guard was down, and nothing in my life reflected that I even believed God existed. I had walked away, turned my back, and was heading down Satan's path instead of

---

[1] *All names have been changed.

God's. I went out with Darius the next day and about every day after. He wanted to be with me all the time and I loved all the attention. It was my first serious relationship. I wanted to be wanted, I wanted to be loved. He liked to get high and drink, but I didn't care, I just wanted to be with someone. I had this huge void in my life and it felt as if it was finally being filled. But there was another side to him. He would push me or grab me so hard I would have finger marks on the inside of my arms almost daily.

The abuse escalated. I had no idea he was smoking crack, but I can look back now and see when his behavior would change and the drugs would make him do things. We would sit in my car behind his house so he could get high on pot, most times I smoked with him. He would light his joint with matches then put them out on my hand or arm and laugh. Sometimes he would just reach over and yank hair out of my head and sometimes he would do it in front of other people. They would be in shock and tell him he was crazy, but rarely did anyone really stand up for me. They knew his behavior was erratic. As I look back, I wonder, why in the world would I stay with someone who did such horrible things to me? Lies, the Devil's lies. Not once did I hear, "You don't deserve this." What I heard was, "It's not that big of a deal. He's just trying to be funny, plus no one else wants you and he loves to spend time with you."

I remember clearly the first time Darius told me he loved me. We were in the car, he was driving and we passed the street my family lived on. I had since moved in with him and his family because my mom gave me an ultimatum, my family or him. I chose him because of the lies in my ear. "She only wants you home so you can babysit for her. She doesn't really care about you."

After a few weeks of living with him, I missed my little sisters and I told him I wanted to visit them. He told me that I couldn't. I was afraid to ask why, but I did anyway.

He said, "Because I love you and I want you all to myself, I don't like sharing you. You are mine."

I couldn't have been happier. He loved me! He finally said he loved me! I had longed to hear those words from a man for as long as I could remember and finally, I heard them! Nothing else mattered.

Now I just had to make sure that he continued loving me. Because I heard a voice that said, "He is the only one who loves you. You don't have anyone else that loves you like he does." He said he loved me so much that his feelings get out of control sometimes and that's why he hit me. He didn't mean it, it was just that he was just scared I would leave him, and it was just an uncontrollable love. I was flattered; no one had ever loved me THAT strongly!

It may be hard for you to comprehend how I could accept that as love, but at that time I was living in such a destructive environment. Love was not something that was being portrayed in any area of my life. I had surrounded myself with people that were on drugs, sold drugs, had family addicted to drugs, family dying from drugs, and dying from aids.

I remember one time, I was heading to Darius' house and a girl I knew through some other people waved my car down. I stopped as she had her son with her who was about two years old. She told me she needed a ride "up the hill," which meant the projects. Let me explain to you the projects in Coatesville, Pennsylvania. There were a few buildings that sat on the top of a hill that overlooked the city. There was only one road that went by them. There was a parking lot at the lower part of the projects, but at the top there was a cul de sac. That meant one way in, and one way out. And not just anyone could drive into that.

It was very dangerous, especially if you were white, because the drug dealers hung out at the top. Different sections sold different drugs. If they didn't know you, they assumed you might be a cop, undercover, or a snitch. Many shootings happened there and cops were gunned down numerous times. My boyfriend would often take me to the lower parking lot late in the night and lock me in the car, taking the keys so I couldn't leave. He would leave me there trapped for hours as he went and got high. I was terrified being surrounded by crack heads and drug dealers, but I had no choice. It was too dangerous for me to try to escape.

As I drove up there with the lady and her son, I was getting nervous. She said it was okay because she would get out and tell the drug dealers I was with her. She got out and told them, and then told me she had to go see a family member to sign a paper. I was scared, knowing anything could happen. Soon, she got back in the car, and within just a few minutes, we were on a back road that led out of that area. She told me she was sorry ... she had lied to me, but she couldn't help it. She then pulled out a crack pipe and started to take some hits of the crack I had just unknowingly taken her to buy. Her little boy was in the backseat, but she said she couldn't help it. She just needed to take a few hits until she could smoke the rest. The smell of crack is so disgusting and hard to describe. It's like smelling metal burning; it makes my stomach turn just to think of the scent. I will never forget that smell. My heart broke for that little boy. I knew there were many other children experiencing the same thing as this child. I always had a soft heart for those in need and this one event stayed with me until my own circumstances overwhelmed my mind again.

I know my grandmother was praying for me then. After she passed away, my mom found a book my grandmother wrote prayers in and it hit me just how much she sought the Lord on our behalf. I'm sure things could've been much worse for me. I never had to be hospitalized for any of the abuse I endured. I did not lose my life. A few times Darius hurt me in front of my sisters and I know it scared them, not knowing what he might do to me. I remember seeing my sister's pain and fear when they saw him treat me badly.

One night, we were in my car, and my sister and her best friend were in the back. We saw his cousin and she needed a ride, but she wouldn't fit and I told him that. He got so angry with me and smacked me across the face in front of all of them. He got angrier and decided he was taking us all back to my mom's house so he could go out with his cousin. He forced my sister and her friend out of the car and dragged me out of the car and threw me down and my body landed on this small fence. He was going to hurt me more, I remember the rage in his eyes, but this man came out of nowhere with a big dog and he was terrified of dogs. The man just stood there, allowing Darius to feel his presence. Darius then decided I had to go with him because he was afraid I'd tell the police. My sister told me not to go with him. She begged me and was crying and screaming, asking why I would be with someone who hurt me. She said she wanted me to just come home and that if I didn't, she wouldn't talk to me anymore.

She couldn't understand how much worse it would get if I *didn't* go with him. I knew they looked up to me and that I was letting them down. I knew I was hurting them, but I felt trapped. I didn't want to hurt them. I wanted to be a good role model, but I wanted to be loved and I thought he would kill me if I tried to leave. And so I stayed.

I look back now and know without a doubt that man and his dog were sent from God. There were so many times the Lord shielded me. He never left me. I had walked away from Him and in spite of that He still protected me that night. I should have died. I could have died that night or the multiple other times he hurt me or left me places where there was no one around. But God's plan cannot be thwarted. I might have been spending all of my time doing what the devil wanted, but God was always available for me to turn to. At any moment, I could have run back into God's loving arms and He would have rejoiced. But I chose to stay on the path I was on. I chose to continually put myself and my family in danger. It was my choice and God never had to protect me because my back was turned.

Another time when he hit me in the face with a basketball and laughed in front of my sister and her friends, I felt shame. I just wanted to hide. I usually tried to play it off and make it seem like it wasn't that big of a deal. And most of the time I didn't tell anyone. It would happen, I would cry, and usually cry myself to sleep or have sex with him to make him happy again, to stop his rage.

On the nights of the abuse, he often took me to his mother's house, dropped me off, took my car and left to get high. He would come home, wake me up, and do what he wanted with me. I would just take my mind somewhere else until he was done. I never imagined that was rape at that time.

One of the times I did try to leave him, he broke out all the windows in my car in front of the place I worked. The police gave me a little pink card that talked about domestic violence and I thought, "*This doesn't apply to me; this is for women who are being abused. I'm not being abused; he loves me and can't control it. That's completely different.*" The lies had taken root deep inside me, and if at any time I started to think otherwise, a voice would tell me differently. "This is as good as it gets for you ... you don't deserve more. Your parents didn't love you and no one else will either."

I moved to a friend's apartment in Northeast Philadelphia, about forty-five minutes away for a few weeks. While I was there, I witnessed a woman being beaten like she was a man, and I witnessed a friend's sister, who was severely addicted to crack and pregnant, try to detox. I wasn't the only one to witness this. There were also two children in the home. My heart broke for those children that saw this often. I knew I'd never let my children live in an environment like that.

Darius' mother told me he was threatening suicide and that he was sick and wouldn't eat because I was gone. She knew what he did and told me if I got pregnant he would change. After all, he was very good with babies. So I believed her. I got pregnant a month or so after and learned how wrong she was.

CHAPTER 7

Out of all the memories of my time with Darius, all the abuse I endured, too many or too graphic to put in a book, or for people to even know about, one time sticks out more than any of the others. This time was different because on this particular night, if it were not for the grace of God, I would be dead. I **know** it was God. I know now it was because of *His* plans for me, for my boys, for my grandchildren, my great grandchildren, and my great great grandchildren! God's plan cannot be stopped by the devil, no matter how many times he tries.

About a week before I found out I was pregnant, he became very mad at me. I didn't want to party with him, because I didn't feel good. Each time I tried to smoke, I would get nauseous and I kept getting headaches. This made him angry because he wanted me to do whatever he was doing at all times. We were in my car arguing about it. I had to work the next day, because it was important that I paid for whatever he needed to support his habit, but he didn't care. His addiction took over and he took off in the car with me still in it. We lived in a city that had lights every mile or so. He drove full speed ahead through four cities, blowing every light, not even pausing at the intersections. I reached down and pulled the lever so my seat went all the way back because I was prepared to die and didn't want to see it coming. I just knew I was going to die and told God, "Please take me, I can't live like this anymore, just please end it, I'm so tired of crying, so tired of the pain. *There is no other way out, Lord, make it all stop.'*

Eventually, we came to a large intersection, each road was one way and it was jam packed. As we got to the intersection, I jumped out of the car and ran and hid. I was crouched down in a fetal position covering my head sobbing. I was praying God would send some strong men or police to help me. Darius found me within what felt like a few minutes. I knew I had no choice but to go with him. I was trapped yet again.

God didn't answer my prayer to take my life that night, but there is no doubt He was with me. I imagine Him holding me in the car, angels surrounding me, blocking out cars that could've hit us head on, or cars we could have run into. There is no reason we didn't get hit or worse! But God was protecting me for a greater purpose I would not even come close to understanding until over a decade later.

Jennifer Munson *Less Than*

I found out a week later that I was pregnant and everything was okay between us for a few weeks. Darius would talk to my belly, put his hands on it and tell the baby he loved him. One morning, I shut his bedroom door the *wrong* way and he grabbed me and threw me hard up against the wall. I was in shock; I thought he had changed now that we were having a baby. His mom started screaming at him telling him he couldn't do that to me. It could hurt the baby. He was too wrapped up in his addiction to have control over his behavior most of the time.

I never went back. I knew I had to choose my baby over him. I already had fresh in my memory what life would be like for me if I stayed and I didn't want my child to grow up thinking that was okay. He threatened my life, my unborn baby's life, and took my car. The police found him and he went to jail. He was incarcerated from October 1994 to April 1995. I wrote to him in prison while I was pregnant and event went to visit him during that time. My son was born June 1995 and Darius went back to jail in October of 1995, after being shot on his front porch by someone he had robbed. He was sentenced to a few years. I went to see him in the hospital; he was left blinded in one eye. I still felt some kind of loyalty to him.

CHAPTER 8

I got my own place in a different town called Phoenixville, about twenty-five miles away from my hometown. The town was very small, and I had only been there a handful of times. I wanted to get away to a place where people didn't know me and associate me with my son's father. I was working full-time for a five star hotel in the Sales and Marketing department. We didn't always have money for food, so we went to the food bank. Sometimes our phone was shut off, but we were on our own. It was not easy.

My son started daycare and realized that the other children had this person they called "daddy." One night, we were lying in bed and he put his hand on my cheek and turned my face to his and said to me, "Mommy, will I ever have a daddy?" Although my son is now eighteen, I can still see that two-year-old's face that night. My heart broke for him and I hated myself for letting him down. I hated myself for choosing such a terrible person to be his father. A father he would never know.

Jennifer Munson *Less Than*

I turned twenty-one and loved being able to go to the bar and get drunk and forget about the cares of the world. On December 23, 1999, we had an office Christmas party. A group of us went to a local bar to dance and drink, and from there I was taken by two guys. They had slipped a drug into my drink and took me to a hotel where one of them worked, and they raped me. I woke up on Christmas Eve day in pain, not knowing where I was, or how I got there, or who did it. I still don't know what they look like, except that one was white and one was black. I can now praise God for not letting me remember the details of that night. I believe He protected me from the memory of what those men did to me.

I spent Christmas night in the ER and the experience was horrible in itself. The doctor treated me as if I was lying because I didn't come in the same night it happened, and the detective was even worse. The policemen who came between those two were very kind to me, but the whole examination, the whole process of what you go through after a rape is so degrading. Having your nails clipped, samples of your hair and skin taken, all while you are trying to make sense of what happened. You are supposed to have a crime victim's advocate with you for the whole procedure, but mine wasn't called early enough and they didn't wait for her. They give you a cup of pills to prevent any disease or pregnancy, which of course I threw up shortly after. It wasn't how I wanted to spend Christmas night. If I had known what you go through reporting rape, I too, would have kept quiet. Later, my advocate told me only one in five rape cases even go to court.

I slipped into depression after that. I couldn't go to my mom for comfort, she just couldn't handle it and that made me feel rejected. The devil's voice was in my ear, "She doesn't believe you or even care what happens to you, because she has never loved you. You aren't good enough. The only people who want you are those who want to use you. You will never be worth more than that." The pain of that rejection hurt so much, and the shame I carried since I was a child became even stronger. I was so angry at God. I thought He would protect me always! I knew I didn't have a relationship with Him anymore, but I thought because I was His child that He would always protect me. I wanted nothing to do with Him. He had let me down, hurt me, and I believed He wasn't the God I was taught about when I was a kid. I was numb and suicidal. It took every ounce of energy in me just to shower or feed my son. I did not feel like I was living, I felt like I was inside someone else's body.

No matter how many others have gone through it, you still feel completely alone, as though the world is going on without you. I felt as if I was standing still and the world was

Jennifer Munson *Less Than*

moving and I wasn't even real. I was seeing a counselor weekly who suggested I write as a way to express my feelings. This poem explains how I felt during this time more than any other words I could give.

January 27, 2000

Where did she go?

It wasn't me that night

The night they robbed me of my soul

It wasn't me that next morning

That morning I awoke feeling less than whole

It wasn't me who smiled the next day

Smiled meaninglessly, just playing a role

It wasn't me who cried straight through that 1st week

That week I realized I had lost my soul

It isn't me now making those jokes

What are jokes anyway?

Jennifer Munson *Less Than*

It isn't me who gets up each morning

Each morning I wake up and pray

It isn't me you see and talk to

The body you see struggling to make it through

You think, I'm that girl that used to laugh and smile

That girl that would always go the extra mile

You think I'm that girl that is always so strong

That girl that never let anything go wrong

You think I'm that girl that can stand up to anything

That girl that used to laugh and sing

You think I'm that girl who doesn't need help

Help she yearns for but won't say it herself

You think I'm that girl that doesn't need someone to hold her

That holding that just hasn't occurred

God do I miss her

Oh how I want her to return

She wouldn't take this pain

Jennifer Munson *Less Than*

She wouldn't let it burn

She would be strong

She wouldn't let this get her down

She'd keep up that smile

And let the pain never be found

But just for right now let her be sad

Just be there for her she needs you so bad

Just for right now hold her so tight

Don't let her go, squeeze with all your might

Just for right now let her be weak

Let her be sad, let her be meek

Just for right now give her your love

Hold her close, make her your cub

Just for right now let her melt in your arms like once again she's your baby

The baby you held, and fed, and loved, and watched grow to be a lady … just for right now

Jennifer Munson *Less Than*

This poem was posted without my name at a local Domestic Violence, and Victims of abuse event. Many girls told my counselor they could relate to what I wrote. I then realized I could be an encouragement someday to others who had endured the same violation.

Working at a hotel with so many strangers coming and going, caused me to live in fear every single day. There were constantly new people arriving and checking out each day. Because I didn't know what those men who raped me looked like and because they were two different races, I thought every man who was white or black could be them and could come back to get me and do it again. The nightmares tormented me night after night. I didn't want to sleep because of the nightmares that came. I was tortured when I was awake and while I slept. Nothing soothed the pain and sadness.

My family doctor gave me anxiety medicine and it helped when I took it. At times I would look at the bottle and wonder if I could take the whole thing. It is only by God's grace that I didn't become addicted to them. God definitely had His hand on me even though I thought the opposite at the time. I always had a fear of drug addiction. I saw how it destroyed people, so I wouldn't allow myself to depend on it. But there is no doubt it is only by God's grace.

Eventually, I realized drinking made me forget and I again could pretend to be someone else. I learned I could say who I would have sex with and use them for it, not giving them the chance to use me. It was an ugly cycle and it went on for longer than I'd even like to admit. I was so overwhelmed with everything-- being a single mom, being responsible for everything and trying to deal with this torment and depression. There were times I would sit at a large intersection and hear a voice tell me to just press on the gas. Wait until a huge truck is coming and just go. End it all. You aren't worth anything, no one loves you, everyone uses you, just end it all. This happened many times over the years. It was a struggle not to do what those voices said.

CHAPTER 9

In 2000, I moved from Pennsylvania to Florida to hide from Darius. He had started writing me, threatening me, right before he got out of prison. He said he had people watching me and that he was going to take my son. I considered changing my name and my son's name, but instead moved to Florida and didn't tell anyone where I was going.

In Florida, I went out every chance I got. I spent many Saturdays hung over on the couch and was not the mom I should have been to my son. He was an angry and frustrated boy. He got in trouble at school almost weekly and his schoolwork suffered. I didn't understand why he was so angry. I thought by letting him do what he wanted, it would make him happy and make up for the fact that I took him from everything he knew. I thought I was doing the right thing by going easy on him, because he didn't have a father and it was my fault. I loved him with everything I had, but didn't know how to show it. I was tormented inside by the rape. I didn't feel alive; I didn't feel like I was living, I did my best not to feel at all.

Jennifer Munson *Less Than*

I tried to keep us fairly isolated, but then I started dating a guy who was a lot of fun, responsible, kind, and we were great friends. He did not believe in God and although I told him we couldn't be in a relationship because of that, we could still "have fun." We had a slip up with our birth control and I got pregnant. I knew I couldn't have this baby, but I also knew I was against abortion. He didn't want the baby and neither did I. We weren't in love and had no desire to make our relationship go past its current level. I decided an abortion was the only way out and it was covered by my health insurance, so for just a fifteen dollar copay I could go back to my life. I felt the guilt sitting in that clinic. I knew it was wrong, I knew it was a lie when they took me into the counseling room and told me it wasn't a life yet. I knew better. I didn't want to be there, but I felt stuck. The waiting room was filled with very young girls, and as a parent, I wanted to tell them all they were making a mistake, but how could I? I sat there filling out the same papers, agreeing to the same thing.

During the procedure, they had to keep reminding me to breathe because I was unconsciously holding my breath. I knew I was killing this life God made inside me. I didn't want to hear that noise as they sucked that little life out. I couldn't cope, so I tried to mentally remove myself from the situation, which caused me to hold my breath. There was a kind woman there whose job was to hold my hand and just be there for me. I wonder now who would sign up for that job, who would say, "That's what I want to be when I grow up." Who wants to listen to that vacuum noise all day every day?

I can't even imagine the torment. I lied to myself to get through it. Immediately after, I asked God to forgive me, that I knew it was wrong. I needed Him to forgive me for killing this baby. I wept to Him, and begged Him for forgiveness for knowing better and making the choice anyway. I numbed it for so long, but it was in my gut, and each time I saw a baby, it hurt me to my core. I had no relationship with God, so I didn't let the feelings stay. I moved forward in my messy life.

CHAPTER 10

I moved back to Pennsylvania in 2003, after my son's father went back to jail for invading someone's home and kidnapping them at gunpoint. My son does not know him. He has asked me if I thought his father had asked Christ into his heart. We pray for him, for God to send someone to him while in jail to tell him about God.

Life was changing for me. I got a great job at a software consulting company. It was a large increase in salary, free health benefits, and unlimited sick time. I also was able to travel to England twice. We were able to move into a large condo that had a fireplace, big bedrooms, and for the first time in my life, I had my own washer and dryer. It felt good to be able to finally live somewhere I wanted, not somewhere I had to settle for. Although this brought temporary happiness, I still felt empty. God always tugged gently at my heart. I would come home from a night out of drinking and feel so alone. Sometimes I contacted churches at night while having one of my crying sessions, and I'd never hear back from them. I'd even visit a church and no one would even say hi, so I wouldn't go back. I did this over a course of nine to ten years.

I would email a pastor, get no response, wait six months, try a new church, no one would \notice me, go another six months, and continue this cycle, each time saying, "See ... God isn't who He says or these people wouldn't be how they are."

My mom gave her life back to the Lord in 2006, and I became angry and frustrated with her. How dare she change into this stuck-up church lady again? How dare she give God a chance, look at what He has done and *not* done for us! I was so angry when she tried to talk to me about God or anything to do with church. I wanted nothing to do with it. I told her she was going through a phase and she would soon be over it, the church was just full of judgmental and self-righteous people.

I did allow her to take my son with her to church, mostly because I was hungover on many Sunday mornings. She started taking my son with her and he got saved, which made me start thinking of how I was raising him and what was I teaching him. I had grown up so strong in the Word as a child and realized he didn't even know who Adam and Eve were. I started really considering church then. I wanted him to know what I knew and realized I was failing him by not teaching him about God. The seed was planted, but did not grow until years later. My stepfather got a job in Florida, so my mom and sister moved with him.

In 2007, I ran into a guy I had dated multiple times in and after high school, Jacob. We fell madly in love. He moved in pretty quickly while my son was visiting my mom in Florida for the summer. I was lonely and always looking for someone or something to fill up all the voids I had, and he did just that.

Soon after we started dating, I found out Jacob smoked weed to help with his anger and depression. Then I found out he had been wanted for a few years for violation of probation. I was not living that lifestyle anymore, but I loved him. Something told me to end it. I already knew what kind of life dating someone who did drugs and ran from the cops led. But those lies in my ear telling me no one would love me like he would, started again. The lies telling me how worthless I was convinced me stay.

He became controlling fast. He didn't want me to wear hardly any makeup and didn't let me wear some of my clothes. I cried, a lot. He would fall asleep and I would sneak out of bed into the living room and cry. I felt trapped and sometimes I would cry to God and ask him to just take him from me. I would tell God I wasn't strong enough to leave him, could he just remove him from my life so that I didn't have to cry so much.

And honestly, God answered my prayer. We got into a big argument and decided to break up. I avoided his calls, avoided seeing him, but the loneliness crept in after just a few days and I gave in. Instead of walking on the path God laid out, I went right back to misery.

I was ashamed that I had somehow ended up in an abusive relationship again, twelve years after I had escaped one. Each time I thought I should try to get out, I'd hear voices saying "You won't do any better; you will never love like you loved Jacob." He'd come back, we'd fight, I'd cry, it was an ugly cycle.

Those of us with imaginations tend to make up scenarios that keep us in the situation we are in no matter how bad it really is. I knew in the moments he was being verbally abusive, I wasn't happy. But I would think if I just do this, or treat him that way, he will change and be a good husband and good father. I would already have this fantasy of a life made up in my head and thought somehow Jacob would fit into that. I would lay my head down at night crying, and to escape the pain I was feeling, I would daydream (pretend, fantasize) about the family I desired. By doing that, it gave me a false sense of hope and I could continue in the bad relationship.

I wanted a husband, a father to my son, someone who really loved me so much that I would make up scenarios in my head of how I wanted life to be and put him in it. I did this often throughout my life; it was a way of coping with the hurt and emptiness I felt most of the time.

Each time, I was hurt and my thoughts would start to drift, and the devil was close by to help me with the lies. I wasn't doing anything to fight him off. Everything I was doing was drawing him closer and inviting him in. The devil is a liar and when you are listening to those lies, you believe them and desire to see them come to pass. "You belong to your father, the devil, and you want to carry out your father's desires. He was a murderer from the beginning, not holding to the truth, for there is no truth in him. When he lies, he speaks his native language, for he is a liar and the father of lies" (John 8:44 KJV).

Jacob had accepted Christ into his heart as a child and suggested we read the Bible and go to church. We read a devotional a few times and he said I was allowed to go to church, and I even got ready one Sunday and picked a church out to go to, but never made it. I let the fear of rejection take over, the little bit of doubt creep in, and the hardness of my heart keep me away. Soon after our talk of church, I got pregnant.

Jacob became more controlling, saying he owned me now. He told me he had another girlfriend and wasn't leaving her, I was now his forever. I told him he was wrong and I wouldn't stay with him. He said he was going to kill me. I left my house, afraid, and he continued to call telling me he was headed to my house and if I wasn't there he would destroy everything in it. He called me almost 100 times within a few hours. I called the police and he left before they got there.

I felt trapped and allowed him back in, but just over a week later we got into a huge argument and he yelled at me in front of my son. I knew it was time to stand my ground. I went to work and he started calling me threatening me that I couldn't leave him. He told me we were going to take a long ride and he'd show me that if I wasn't going to be his, I wasn't going to be anyone's. He threatened to kill me again and told me that my only other option to not be with him would be if I got an abortion, but that he would have to be there to make sure I went through with it. I called the police, and told them about the warrant and they found him walking towards my house. They cuffed him and made me drive to where he was to identify him before taking him to jail.

There I was pregnant again, alone again, broken and tired again. How could I have another child who wouldn't have a father? I already knew the pain and void it left.

My mom was praying so hard for me. I told her I didn't want to have this baby, and she said, "Jenn, maybe this child will cure cancer. You don't know the plans the Lord has for this child. You can't get rid of this baby."

I knew she was right. She kept sending me Bible verses from the book of Isaiah and it always seemed to talk about strength. Naming him Isaiah reminded me of the strength God gave me to get through that time, even though I was still His prodigal daughter.

CHAPTER 11

I had my baby in May of 2008. He was sick a lot and he cried so much, and I cried so much. He spent a week in the hospital when he was seven weeks old. They didn't know what was wrong with him, and he wasn't getting better. I was so afraid I would lose him. I remember asking my mom to pray, because I knew God would hear her since she had a relationship with Him. I wasn't sure God would hear me. I remember thinking, I could pray and ask God to heal my son, but it would be a lie if I told Him I was going to turn my life around if He did. I felt very alone during that time, my mom had moved to Florida and my older son was visiting her for the summer. They never found out what was wrong with him but he did start to get better.

Isaiah didn't start sleeping through the night until he was two years old. He had silent reflux, which led me to my love for Chiropractic. That was the only thing that gave him relief. I was so tired all the time. I got laid-off in April 2009, and in July 2009, I had been having pain spread through my body daily and was diagnosed with chronic Lyme Disease. This is a controversial disease; it takes your muscles, including the ones in your brain and weakens them. I would forget words, forget where I was, see things running across the floor, and wake up and not be able to move.

With Lyme you were only allowed (by law) to get treated with antibiotics in very high dosages. Blood work is done often to make sure the liver was handling all the medications. Everything had to be written down because I couldn't remember if I took my medication. So my calendar became my best friend. Everything was written on it.

I was lying on the couch one day and said out loud, "God, I know what you are trying to do, you are trying to get me back, and I'm telling you, it will not work." Well, that was the wrong thing to say! Soon after, I tried to walk from one room to another and would get stuck in a certain position, unable to move. I would be in the middle of a sentence and forget a simple word. I would drive down a street I'd been on a thousand times and forget where I was. I felt powerless.

The thing is, I didn't look sick. There is no way to explain what that feels like. On the outside, you look normal, but on the inside all you feel is pain twenty-four hours a day. It was debilitating and I was depressed, sick, and lonely. No work, no health, and little help. I was down to nothing. I was stripped of everything. I had nowhere to turn but to Jesus.

I started reading my Bible here and there, praying here and there. My mom had gotten me to start reading the Tribulation series and it talked about Christ returning and that put some fear in me and also some hunger to know God again. I went to a church I had been eyeing. I was really starting to feel passion again about having a relationship with God. I was so happy to be there. The greeters said hello, asked if I was a single mom and I said yes. They told me they had "others" like me. I liked the service, no one said hi to me other than the greeter, but I went back that night. No one said hi to me, but I went to the juice and cookie reception after the evening service and stood in line to get my juice and cookies with my son. No one said hi to me as I stood in line for 15-20 minutes. No one said hi to me as I stood there alone eating a cookie and drinking juice. No one stopped me on my way out. I never went back.

These encounters always made me wonder where the love of God was. If it isn't being shown in a church, where would I feel and see it? How can it be real?

CHAPTER 12

My mom came into town for Christmas. I had asked her to buy me a NIV Bible and she did, along with a devotional book to read. She gave me another book about a local evangelist who was a former drug dealer and gang leader. It was used and had been passed around by people who had been touched by his story. I threw it aside for a few weeks and kept looking at it rolling my eyes. I finally picked it up and read about Jose Perez, who had a terrible life, was a terrible man, and how he would have these encounters with people and have visions. I read how God had changed his life and about supernatural things I was never told about before that he said was in the very Bible I grew up reading. I still wasn't sold on his story though, after all I'd heard plenty of stories growing up about drug dealer turning in to preachers.

Out of curiosity, I went to his website thinking he probably didn't even have a ministry anymore. After all, his book was kind of old. There was a video on his website; it was a recording of him preaching in the ghetto. He was sweating, yelling his testimony of how Christ saved him and changed him, and about how he should have died many times.

There were tons of people coming forward to be saved. I started crying, my body trembled, and I had goose bumps all over. This peace overwhelmed me, and every worldly desire of music, cursing, and everything else I went after was completely gone. I didn't understand. I knew without a doubt I had prayed to be saved when I was 5, but I felt like it happened again. I was confused but also so happy. I emailed the church thinking I wouldn't hear back, and the next day they emailed me and said they were praying for me and asked if they could call me. Another woman emailed me and invited me to church, one woman called me and told me her testimony and prayed with me over the phone.

I drove over an hour to the church in Northeast Philadelphia. The first Sunday, I was greeted and hugged in the parking lot, then again within steps of walking in the doors. I had told them what happened when I was on the website, and they explained I had been baptized in the Holy Ghost. I had no idea what it meant. I slowly learned, and was overwhelmed by the emotions I felt at church that I had never felt before. There was a song that talked about God making the broken whole again and that explained exactly how I felt. I was so broken because of my past and I wanted to be made whole. I was hungry for it!

At every service I attended, I shed tears. God was restoring my soul. I was still struggling with Lyme disease and the effect it was having on my body. I spent an hour a day in a detox bath, and during that time, I would pray and read *Beauty for Ashes* by Joyce Meyer. I learned that sometimes we go through things alone so the Holy Spirit can truly be our guide, our teacher, our friend, and our counselor. Sometimes our voids are filled with people when that void must be filled with God first. I learned that He wanted to take my broken pieces and make me whole again. I learned that He was always waiting to take me back. He loved me even though I had ignored Him for years.

I decided to move to Florida to be closer to my mom and sister so I could have help with my sons. I struggled with leaving my church, because it was the first place that I felt like I was accepted and where I was growing. After praying, I decided it was the best thing to do. I moved in May 2010 and started the hunt of finding a new church.

CHAPTER 13

I met a guy who went to a large church and I started going to Sunday school with him. I had not dated in years. I knew that men were always a downfall for me. But he was a Christian, so I thought it was okay. I learned that just because someone says they are a Christian does not mean their heart is after God like mine. I had never dated a Christian before, and I was naïve. I chose to continue to spend time with him and slowly started to let my values fade. One week I would stand firm and the next week I'd give in. I had a void that was now being filled by a person instead of God, but didn't realize it.

I met others around my age and started going to Worship before Sunday School and also to other groups on other nights. I was growing in the Lord and my hunger for Him stayed strong. I was learning so much and remembered things I had been taught when I was young, but it meant something different to me now. I was learning to forgive and learning that I had to be healed to truly move forward.

In April of 2012, my life changed forever. I am choosing not to give the details of what happened. But I was hurt from inside the church. This hurt was worse than anything previously done to me in life. It knocked me to my knees and I knew without a doubt the devil was trying to get me back to his world. I told him out loud this time, "I see what you are trying to do and it won't work." I had nowhere to turn, but up. I was in so much pain and asked God why He gave me this. "Out of the thousands of members at that church, why me, Lord? How can this happen inside a church? I am going there for healing, I am going there to grow and change. How, Lord, does this evil take place where people come to be healed from past hurts? I'm a single mom, and my mom can't handle stuff like this." I was always told to forget and move on. But I knew the Lord didn't want that. I tried to find books, websites, people that would have advice as to why this happened. How can this happen, why would God allow this? If everything goes through His hands first, where was He that day? Why didn't He protect? Wasn't He watching? Why didn't He stop this from happening?

I worked with an amazing godly woman who stopped at my desk while at work and asked "How are you really doing?" and I broke down telling her I looked like I was coping on the outside but inside I was falling apart. She asked if I would speak to her friend and promised not to tell her anything. I agreed and just a few days later met this woman on my lunch break at a park. I sat down and she handed me a paper that I still have today, that said this;

"I asked God what He might want to say to you today and this is what He said, 'I have not left you child, though it seems you are alone and feeling swallowed up by the circumstances. You can't hear me now, but you will feel me well, says the Lord. Things will happen to make you question my love for you, but I will never leave you nor forsake you in times of trouble. My hand is upon you always and I will vindicate the righteous ones.

"Solomon was a man of honor, and his armies fought for the cause, but in time, he turned his eyes from me and was swept away in the sea of his own choices. Clarity will come as you rest in willingness to let me heal your heart, but don't be led away by your mind, trying to understand why. A time is coming where you will understand that I have the ability to set all thing right for my glory. You will rise from the ashes of despair and I will make you an example of my provision and grace. Nothing is too big for me to handle, nothing. I love you, Papa.'"

As I sat weeping at the timeliness of each precious word and feeling God closer than I had ever felt Him before, I wondered how she heard from Him like that, and also wondered if it was possible for me. And if it was, how could I make it happen. I wanted to hear and feel Him like that over and over, and so I began to seek Him with every ounce of my being. I struggled daily to get past the pain and wondering why this happened to me.

I went to a family I trusted and told them what happened, asking to please tell me why and how. This wise man of God sat silent for a few moments and then he said very calmly but with authority, "Jenn, I don't know the answers to your questions, and I don't know why things like this happen. But what I do know is that when we suffer, we become more like Jesus." Wow! I knew I wanted to be more like Him. The more time I spent with God, the more I understood that statement, but it wasn't overnight.

I was still in so much pain and crying out to the Lord asking why did I have to go through this by myself. No one was with me at night stroking my hair telling me it would be okay, or hushing me as I cried. No one was hugging me when I was falling apart and feeling as if I couldn't go another day. No one was saying let me help you, let me take the burden off you; or let me ease the pain just a bit. I would hold myself together all day feeling as if I was going to burst if I didn't allow the tears to flow. Sometimes I would get in the shower just so I could go in there and cry and lean against the wall begging for God to carry me, to give me the strength to put on a smiling face for my sons.

As soon as my sons went to bed, I would get on my knees in the living room with my Bible before me and sob to the Lord. "Okay God, you want me to be like you, but why alone Lord? Why must I do this alone?"

He answered. I heard Him tell me as clearly as if He sat next to me, "If you had someone, if you had a person to go to, than you wouldn't come to Me. I am your source. I am your true and only source to happiness, your true and only source of healing, your true and only source to love. I am your source for everything, and the only source needed. I can meet every single need in every area of lack. I give you what no human can and what I give is lasting."

I was so desperate for God. I started to pray, most of the time crying asking Him to heal me. I asked Him to show me my weak areas, to teach me and show me the way. I asked for the Holy Spirit to guide me. I went to a very small church of about 15 people on Saturday nights. Most of the time, I would just cry and then go home, put my son to bed and spend time with God. I called them date nights with Jesus. I was getting to know Him again; I was in a new relationship with Him. Many Saturdays, I would be on my knees with God's Word in front of me and I would cry and beg Him to heal me, show me what to do, and what to read to heal and be changed. I would pray for God to protect my boys, but I didn't trust that He would.

CHAPTER 14

God needed to do some work inside of me. I started to hear from Him very clearly and often. Each time I heard Him, I wanted more. I would turn off my radio on the way to work so I could talk to Him and hear Him. I couldn't wait for my lunch break so I could sit in my car with my Bible and my journal to write everything He said. I could feel Him lifting the hurt, bits at a time. God told me He loved me with an unfailing love, that His mercy never fails and that I'm fearfully and wonderfully made by Him, and *He's God*! He told me the road I have traveled, the hardships, the battles, have brought me exactly where He wants me. God told me that He loves me so much that He has taken me right to the exact place I'm at. He promised to give me back one hundred more blessings than I can imagine. He promised to restore to me the years the locust had eaten. He promised me that I would be exceedingly happy. But I must keep doing His will and *focusing* on Him.

I learned that although trials can be long and intense, I had to wait on God to act in His timing even when it feels like I can't. God took an oath in His name, and my hope is secure

Jennifer Munson *Less Than*

and immovable. I must stay anchored in God. He wanted to change my heart and had already tried over and over, but I kept saying "no, I don't trust you, no I'm not ready." He wanted all of me and told me it was time to give it all over to Him, every single area, every single hurt, every pain, every abuse. He wanted me to hand it all over. God started transforming me after I surrendered everything to Him. It's like I had locks on all these areas of struggle, and He didn't fight me for the key. God waited for me to hand it over to Him and let Him in. I needed to let God open up those locked up places in me and take out the bad and replace it with His goodness.

The Lord gave me a vision of a water pitcher, which represented me. I saw the water pitcher being broken into hundreds of pieces because of what life brought, and everything inside came rushing out. Then God took those pieces, picked them up one by one, and placed each piece in place gluing the pitcher back together with His love. After the pieces were in their exact places, the pitcher was made whole again, because of God's love. It was now a beautiful and useable tool. It represented Him and everything inside was now of God. Anything poured out of it would be of God, and it would no longer have the nasty, ugly, messy things of the world inside. But first, it had to broken, so it could be made beautiful in its time. I had to be broken to be made brand new again.

Giving up control was not easy for me. I like to have control; giving others control in my past had not worked well for me. God showed me I had to rest in Him. I had to stop doing so much on my own, trying to analyze everything, trying to figure out why the bad happened, and instead allow growth and transformation to happen while I rested in Him.

The closer I got to God, the more the devil tried to bring up the past to make me sad. I remembered things my mom said to me that hurt so bad or what men had said or did to me. These memories made me feel worthless and reminded me of that feeling that I was less than everyone else.

I would weep and ask, "Why, Lord? Why did You give me this life? I know You want me to be more like You, I know You are trying to change me; I know that You have great plans for me, but does it have to be so difficult? Does this road have to be so lonely and the struggle so long?"

Jeremiah 29:1 reads, "And ye shall seek me, and find *me*, when ye shall search for me with all your heart" (KJV).

CHAPTER 15

I started going to a church where the Pastor had a passion for bringing people off the streets, discipling them, teaching them how to fight and be successful for the kingdom of God. My Pastor encouraged me to write my story, and I tried before, but each time I attempted to write I became overwhelmed with sadness. It was so painful to relive the memories of the things I had endured. I tried one more time and felt the Lord telling me that as I write, things would be revealed and as He revealed them to me, He would also heal me from them.

I started writing, thinking I had remembered everything, but I was wrong. I remembered things I can't put in writing and it made me sob. My heart felt as if it was breaking in two. I thought, *No, Lord, I can't take anymore!* He said to me, "My girl, as you remember each pain, each hurt, lay them at My feet. The price has been paid. Jesus suffered for every tear you shed, so hand it over and lay them at the cross."

You see, as I write this book, I have been laid off from a great job and unemployment has run out. I am living with no income. I received my first eviction notice on my door in November last year. As I opened it up and read "You are indebted to us for this amount," I started to cry. It made me realize I should have an eviction notice from God for all the wrong I had done and for all the years I had turned away from Him. But instead, He takes each one of my eviction notices and stamps them saying, "PAID IN FULL." Jesus paid my debt of sin! Jesus took my eviction notice with Him and said, "I will sacrifice my life so you can be free." In spite of everything I have done, because of His love He offered up His life. It is up to me whether I act like it or not. It is up to me whether I live like it or not. It is up to me whether I share my story so others can know the price has been paid, the victory has been won, and we must claim it.

Just imagine winning the lottery, a million dollars, and knowing the money was available, and all you had to do was show up and say it's yours! But instead, choosing not to pick it up and claim it, continuing to live in poverty all the while knowing you could live like a millionaire, but choosing to stay poor. That is what we do when we don't live in the freedom that has been paid for by Jesus' sacrifice of His life on the cross. If I continue to live in bondage. continue to be a slave to my thoughts, to my job, to bad relationships, to addictions, I am choosing to stay weighed down by the things of this world, even though Jesus has made it possible for me to be free. One of my favorite chapters in the Bible is Galatians 5, verse 1 says, "It is for freedom that Christ has set us free. Stand firm, then, and do not let yourselves be burdened again by a yoke of slavery."

He's done it. He's made it so I can be free, and it is up to me to stay free. It is up to me to claim my freedom and to not go back (do not let yourselves be burdened again).

CHAPTER 16

My Pastor told me I could make an appointment if I wanted to meet with her for a deliverance session. I knew I needed it, but wasn't sure how it worked or what happened. Before our appointment I prayed and the Holy Spirit told me to fast and pray beforehand. I knew I was going into battle and I wanted to be equipped and willing to be set free. I wanted my flesh to be weakened so my spirit could rise up, so I chose to fast before my appointment. My flesh fights my spirit and when I fast, it is weakening my fleshly desires so I can focus on strengthening my spirit.

Fasting is another weapon God gives me that I often overlooked. I fast often now as I understand what power it holds. God gave me a vision one day as I was fasting and walking on the beach seeking God's presence. When I had walked away from God for all those years, people would tell me that I was like a turtle. That each time someone got close, I would go into my protective shell where I thought I was safe and no one could get me. God showed me that day that fasting was also like a turtle, because when I fast, it's a way of putting my flesh away (into the shell) and allowing my spirit to be the outer protective shell. My spirit takes over my flesh and becomes strong and the flesh submits because it has been weakened. I then realize what my spirit needs; I can hear the Holy Spirit more clearly, because I have denied the desires of my flesh.

Matthew 6:16 says, "Moreover when ye fast, be not, as the hypocrites, of a sad countenance: for they disfigure their faces, that they may appear unto men to fast. Verily I say unto you, they have their reward." Notice it says WHEN you fast, not IF. This is a tool God has given me; it is a weapon against the forces of evil. Why have Christians fallen away from using this valuable tool? If I am going into a boxing ring, I sure wouldn't leave my boxing gloves at home! I refuse to let the weapons God has given me be left at home in some closet. So when it was time for me to clean out my "house," I was ready.

At my deliverance appointment, it was explained to me about the different demons, evil spirits, and principalities and how they can enter. I had never heard of some of them. I had never heard any preaching on such things. I was told what to read and where to go in the Bible. It was explained why we need deliverance, what strongholds did to our lives, how generational curses are passed down, and how soul ties can keep us in bondage. I could quickly and easily look back at the same pains, struggles, failures that had happened to me, my mom, my grandmother, and knew without a doubt I did not want to pass it down to my children and great grandchildren.

There are a few reasons why I am going to go into detail as to what happened at the times I had deliverance. The first reason is because it is not talked about enough. The second reason is because the devil does not want people to have the knowledge nor does he want them to believe it. In Hosea 4:6, the first part of the verse says, "My people are destroyed for lack of knowledge…" (KJV) You've heard that saying "What you don't know, can't hurt you." That's a lie. What you don't know can kill you. The Word of God tells us that.

I am giving you my first-hand account of what I went through. Whether you believe me or not is your choice. I choose freedom, I choose God's Word. I choose to believe what He says, not what some preacher has told me or what I have been told to believe. I have learned to read the Bible and seek guidance from the Holy Spirit and ask God for revelation. I don't want to perish because of my lack of knowledge.

There are many verses in the Bible that tell me that the Word of God is a weapon. It won't do me any good if I'm not opening it up. This is the vision I had, if someone broke into my home and started to come after me and I had a knife in my pocket, I sure wouldn't leave it there. I would take it out and use it to fight, to defend my life! Leaving it in my pocket would do me no good, no matter how sharp, no matter how big, in my pocket it would not ward off my enemy. I have the Word of God to fight off the devil! We must memorize the Scriptures and learn how to use them.

Hebrews 4:12 states, "For the word of God is quick, and powerful, and sharper than any two-edged sword, piercing even to the dividing asunder of soul and spirit, and of the joints and marrow, and is a discerner of the thoughts and intents of the heart." Another verse that tells me God's Word is my weapon is Ephesians 6:17. "And take the helmet of salvation, and the sword of the Spirit, which is the word of God:" It's a sword!! It was written so I could use it against attacks of the enemy!

CHAPTER 17

My Pastor read Psalm 91 over me and prayed, covering us in the blood of the lamb. I closed my eyes as she prayed. I lifted my hands in surrender and as she prayed against past hurts and people who had hurt me, I started crying. She started to identify spirits that were attacking me, the strongest being the spirit of rejection. I felt a stirring inside me as if I was fighting something. I felt my hands wanting to clench and I was getting angry. In my spirit, I kept telling it to leave. This spirit told my pastor it belonged there, that I was its home because it had been there since I was a little girl. My pastor claimed authority over it in Jesus' name and told it that it did not belong there and the blood of Jesus covered me. After some time, it finally agreed to come out telling her it would only come back in when I left the office. She then called out sexual demons that had entered from abuse. As she was calling them out, the struggle inside was strong, the stirring was heavy and I started to scream and yell at the same time. It's hard to describe what was coming out of me; it was like a violent wailing. I could feel the internal struggle. I could feel the anger and torment of the evil spirit and even the fear. A mucus type of substance that smelled like vomit came from my nose. When it was all over, I was exhausted from the struggle and from these spirits that had taken up residence in me for so long it felt like I just had surgery. I was dizzy and extremely tired, and I eventually walked out of the office, and as I was leaving, I suddenly felt very sad and felt sorry for myself and wanted to sit down and cry. I heard the Holy Spirit tell me to rebuke the spirit of rejection and to continue to pray and continue to fast. I got into my car and heard the Holy Spirit say not to turn on the radio, my mind must not get distracted and I must pray the entire way home.

As I was driving, everything looked brighter and clearer, as if I had sunglasses on my entire life and they had just been taken off for the first time. Was the sky always this blue? The clouds so white? I was also very aware of the evil out there, the spirits that were around. I got home and kept praying and had to lay down from being so exhausted from this cleansing that had just occurred. I felt this overwhelming sense of love and lightness. I felt as if weights were taken off of me.

I wanted to go get my two boys out of school and tell them how much I loved them. I wanted to just be with them. I shamefully had never felt love for them that strongly before. I realized I never knew how to love them as they should be.

The spirit of rejection had taken up residence in me, lying to me for so long, in fact my whole life, I never knew what it felt like to actually love someone as God intended. Of course I loved my children, but not how I was supposed to. I changed as a mom. I wanted to do more for them to show them my love. The things I did before at times were only because I was supposed to as a mom, not just because I loved them. I made them dinner because that's what moms do. I picked them up from school because that was my responsibility. What changed is that I wanted to do those things because I loved them, not because it was expected of me.

When I attended church that next Sunday, I was in awe as soon as the worship team started to sing. I looked around to see if anyone else noticed. Everyone was singing as usual as if nothing was happening. I could not believe how good they sounded. I mean they sounded like professional singers! It blew me away! I always thought they sounded good, but now they sounded out of this world. And when I sang and praised God, it felt different. All along, those evil spirits had distorted the music and praise, and now I was free! I couldn't wait to see what else changed.

After the service, a few people told me that I looked like I had a glow about me, as if my eyes were brighter and my skin was bright. I praise the Lord every single day for restoring me. I cry in adoration to the Lord almost every single day for opening my eyes and healing me. He is so worthy of all my praises. If He gave me nothing else for the rest of my life, He is still worthy of all my praise and all my worship!

After my first deliverance, my thinking changed drastically about many things. I was able to regain some memories I had blocked, and also admit to many things I did and shouldn't have done. I realized how much pain and worry I had caused many people over the years. I was ashamed of how I was as a sister. I was the sister the family worried would end up dead. I caused fear, anxiety, and many tears. I had to ask for forgiveness for all the pain I caused. No matter what happened to me that made me that way, I still chose to take the actions I did and am responsible for them. I praise God for wiping my slate clean and forgiving me.

CHAPTER 18

Once I went through deliverance, I had to take steps to stay free. There are steps to help me continue to claim the victory over my life. Many verses tell me to renew my mind (Romans 12:2). In 2 Corinthians 10:5, it says I should be, "Casting down imaginations, and every high thing that exalteth itself against the knowledge of God, and bringing into captivity every thought to the obedience of Christ;" James 4:7 tells me that I can rebuke Satan and hear God. "Submit yourselves therefore to God. Resist the devil, and he will flee from you."

A few months went by, and I continued reading my Bible daily, spending hours with God, fasting and praying. I loved just being in His presence, seeking His face, wisdom, and guidance. I wanted to be a strong warrior for God. I knew I needed more deliverance and set up another appointment with my Pastor.

I expected the same thing to happen. It didn't. Nothing manifested and I felt let down, I didn't understand.

Over the next few days, I kept hearing these voices telling me I was never going to be loved by a man, and that I was going to be alone forever. They even said I wasn't a good mom; I had made too many mistakes. I also heard the voices telling me going to church was pointless, and that I should just give up.

I would cry and say "No! I know this is the devil." I would pray, read my Bible, sing praise songs and they would leave and quickly come back. I couldn't make them stop. I thought of sending my Pastor a message, but heard "She's busy, you can wait." Then heard "You should be strong enough to handle this on your own. She will think less of you if you tell her what you are hearing and feeling." So I went another day hearing these voices and basically just crying. I would be cooking dinner and just start crying because these voices were telling me how worthless I was. My five-year old was telling me that he didn't want me to cry so much. Why did I always cry?

It was a Friday night around 8:00 p.m. and I typed up the message to my pastor and then was going to delete it, but hit send by accident. Within minutes, my Pastor responded, "Meet me at the church."

I was shocked, but thought maybe she was there already or had happened to be going there; certainly she wouldn't go just for me.

I got there around 9:00 p.m. She was outside talking to one of the member's husbands and I walked inside and there were a few others there. I didn't understand what was going on. Then some of our prayer team showed up and we were told to go into the sanctuary and to start praying. I couldn't even stop crying long enough to pray a whole sentence. I wanted to tell them that I couldn't pray. I was too weak! I am losing the battle!

One of my sisters in Christ was telling us to come on and pray, that this was serious; we were praying for our county and praying against witches and curses being sent out to destroy people.

Our pastor came in and told us how a few of us were experiencing the same attacks at the same time and had contacted her. I went up for prayer and she called out the spirit of schizophrenia. I had never thought once that I had schizophrenia. Not one time in my life did I ever think that what I heard in my ear all those years was a voice that wasn't mine. Not once. I had been deceived by the father of lies.

Jennifer Munson *Less Than*

I am going to describe this from my viewpoint, because after all, that's all I know. This evil spirit of schizophrenia did not want to come out. I was on my knees and the evil spirit was slamming my hands on the floor, very angry. Each time my pastor said, "The blood of Jesus," my ears burned. It was so painful to hear those words; the evil spirit knew how much power it had. The evil spirit would try to cover up my ears so I couldn't hear. The Pastor and prayer team had to keep pulling my hands down from my ears. This evil spirit kept saying, "Nooo! Nooo! I don't want to go!" I was shaking my head back and forth to say no. It was very stubborn and angry and had me looking around for objects I might be able to get a hold of and hurt the people praying for me. I had to fight it, because I did not want to hurt them. I could feel the fear it had of leaving and it knew the power of the name and blood of Jesus. Some other ones were expelled also, which came out in the form of vomiting. It was a long process. I was on my knees for quite some time.

I understood that just because I was saved did not mean my flesh couldn't be attacked by evil spirits. I cannot be possessed as the Holy Spirit lives inside me, but my flesh can have evil spirits that take control and that is why I struggle with things like lustful thoughts, addictive behavior, cursing, lying, depression, the list can go on and on.

After it was over, I was extremely exhausted. I went to bed feeling as if I had just run twenty miles. I woke up and started praying as I always do, thanking God for giving me another day. I realized it was just me talking. I realized for the very first time in my life that my mind was completely quiet and at peace. When I had thoughts, they were only mine and were so clear and decisive. I had never experienced this. I had no idea before that day that's how it supposed to be. I did not realize that what I had heard for thirty eight years was not supposed to be there. Let me explain it this way. Imagine being color blind, but not knowing it. No one ever told you that everyone else saw things in color. You always saw everything in black and white and didn't know there was anything wrong with that. Then one day, you receive prayer and you open your eyes and see red, black, green, yellow, purple, pink, and orange, or blue for the first time. Can you imagine how shocked you would be? Can you imagine how you would praise God? Can you imagine how you would want to tell others? Can you imagine how your view of the world would now be completely different than how you had ever seen it before? Can you imagine how angry you might be, frustrated and want to fight to always see color, not just black and white because you feel as though you have been robbed and lied to your entire life up until that point?

For me, God has finished it. He has healed me completely, blessed be the Name of the Lord!

Epilogue

I am angry at the devil! I am extremely mad that he has stolen close to forty years of my life and thoughts. I am so angry that he robbed me of so much. He robbed my children of so much. So please understand I am on a mission to take back what the enemy has stolen. And to do my best not to let him have any more of what is *rightfully* mine.

One of the purposes of sharing my testimony is to encourage others to share theirs. One time, as I was shopping at the supermarket, I saw a girl on the phone, rummaging through the discount bakery items. I heard the Holy Spirit say "give her twenty dollars." Now, let me make it clear that I do not just go around giving strangers money, but I knew I had to obey. She was still talking on her phone and I heard her say, "Mom, I don't have enough to even get my daughter a cake. She's such a good girl; I just want to celebrate her getting on the honor roll." She cried as she talked. I interrupted her and put the money in her hand and asked if I could pray with her. She started crying answering with a "yes". I prayed with her as the Holy Spirit filled me with the words that she needed to hear. She shared how she had felt so

Jennifer Munson *Less Than*

alone and as if no matter how hard she tried, her life was always so difficult. I knew oh so well how that felt. I shared some of my testimony with her telling her that God had not forgotten her and loved her so much and a plan and a purpose for her life. I asked if I could have her phone number so I could continue to encourage her. I praised God for changing me and allowing me to be a vessel of His love.

The devil deceives us into thinking we should be ashamed of our past, which keeps us from sharing how He has changed us. He accuses us of the wrongs we have done, but God says in His Word that we are overcomers (to overcome: to get the better of in a struggle or conflict. To prevail over, to overpower). If we are not telling anyone of how God has changed us, we are not testifying of God's power, grace, and mercy. What was the point of our past struggles and sins that we overcame if we are not telling how God brought us out of it? Our testimony is living proof that God transforms, redeems, restores, and saves!

We are given testimonies for the purpose of glorifying God. When we are saying words that glorify God, I imagine the devil feeling as if he got kicked in the stomach! I imagine as we open up our mouths to tell how great God is, because of what we used to do and how he has changed us, the devil comes into our ear saying, "You should be ashamed of yourself." When we rebuke him, the devil must get angry, because we have overcome him once again and brought glory to God.

> Revelation 12:10-11 " And I heard a loud voice saying in heaven, Now is come salvation, and strength, and the kingdom of our God, and the power of his Christ: for the accuser of our brethren is cast down, which accused them before our God day and night. And they overcame him by the blood of the Lamb, and by the word of their testimony; and they loved not their lives unto the death."

Each situation, test, and trial that God has allowed, is ultimately pointing towards His love. It's a chance for you to know Him as your redeemer, your savior, healer, restorer, Lord, master, husband, father, and so on. I want to know God and experience Him for all that He is. I was thinking about all the names He has, and recently looked them all up, and then prayed He would reveal Himself to me as each of those. I also know that praying this could bring undesirable situations. But God is the lover of my soul, the lifter of my head. "But thou, O LORD, art a shield for me; my glory, and the lifter up of mine head" (Psalm 33:3 KJV).

He has rescued me over and over and I want to know Him in every way. The amazing thing is He desires just as much of me. No matter how many mistakes I have made, or will make, He will always desire all of me. He will always want a more intimate relationship with me. The Bible tells us that He is a jealous God. He doesn't want anything taking His place or coming before Him. Some situations had to happen in my life so I could know Him and seek Him first.

I am so thankful for the spiritual mother God brought into my life during this time. People often question the need for church, "Why do we need church? I can watch it online." If I had not sought out a church and a pastor who were truly seeking God, I do not believe I would have gotten deliverance. You cannot get that by watching it on TV, because relationships cannot be developed over a television.

The devil seeks to isolate us because then we are vulnerable to his attack. When you have a pastor that is seeking God at all times then you will learn by their example, their wisdom and knowledge will trickle down to you so that you might experience freedom.

One reason I chose to share this is because I did not know personally what a true Shepherd was. "Where no counsel is, the people fall: but in the multitude of counsellors there is safety" (Proverbs 11:14). The godly woman God brought into my life has taught me so much, and her unconditional love and guidance is priceless. She has learned from her own mistakes and trials and instead of hiding it, she pours into other people. I thank God she fights to do God's will. It is people like her who truly fight the good fight that inspire me to do the same.

I also want to take time to thank my mom. She has been a prayer warrior for many years in the midst of her own testing and trials. Many times, she offered words of wisdom and I didn't take them. Many times, she offered advice and I did not receive it because of the spirit of rejection clouding my ears. I am thankful for her beyond words and respect her faithfulness to God. Each memory of pain, abuse, rejection, and neglect that God allowed me to remember to write this book was painful beyond words. It hurt so much that I would stop writing for months, it was too painful. I'd stop and tell God, "It's too much, please stop, I don't want to remember anything else!" But what I realized is, each time I remembered something that was so painful it took me weeping to my knees, I cried out to my Savior. I cried out to my healer, I cried out to the lifter of my head. He reminded me that each pain, and all my suffering had already been paid for on the cross. I had to remember the blood, and the nail pierced hands that paid for it all. Then I had to accept the healing blood, the cleansing blood, the atoning blood, the blood that washes me white as snow. Each of us has a Kinsman Redeemer named Jesus. He bought us with a price.

I have struggled with how to end this book. You see, as I write this, I owe three months of rent, three months of car payments, both of which can be gone in a week. Both things which already should have been taken. But thank God, they haven't. My electric is not paid, my water is not paid. If one of my sons needed a pair of shoes at this moment, I could not buy them for him. I struggled with sharing this, because my flesh said what a sad ending to your book. But honestly, I have never felt freer. You see, I can't take care of my finances currently. I have applied for hundreds and hundreds of jobs. I have had great interviews, but until God wants me in a position, I won't get it. God is my provider for everything. If I need something, anything, I ask Him for it. I am dependent on Him in every way.

I have to pray every day that I am fully satisfied with the "bread" He gives me for the day and am not anxious for tomorrow. No earthly treasure can give me what God gives me. No shopping trip, no piece of clothing or jewelry can satisfy my needs any longer. I've experienced a fullness that can only come from my Abba Father.

Some days I cry out to Him and tell Him it's too hard. But then I remember, He has written every day of my life before I came about, and I can rest in that.

Hebrews 10:23 says, "Let us hold unswervingly to the hope we profess, for HE WHO PROMISED IS FAITHFUL. God can not lie, He promises to take care of my needs and so my hope stays in Him, and in the promises of His word." Psalm 73:26 , "My flesh and my heart may fail, BUT GOD…"

I pray that God meets you in your time of need. I pray this book touches you exactly how it's meant to. God loves you, my dear friend, and He has not forgotten you. He desires all of you. He wants to take you to higher levels of worship, higher levels of praise, higher levels of intimacy with Him, higher levels of knowledge and wisdom. But first you must say yes. You must seek Him. And when you seek Him with all your heart precious child of God, you shall find Him.

Don't get stuck in the torment and self-condemnation of your wrong choices. Turn to God, who has already forgiven you, and ask Him to guide you. Experience freedom, joy, and peace that comes from being in God's presence. , "Send for your light and your truth, let them guide me; let them bring me to your holy mountain, to the place where you dwell" (Psalm 43:3 NIV). It took me twenty years to seek Him fully, but once I did He opened up His arms and grabbed me and I refuse to ever go back to who I was. Refuse today to let the devil have one more moment of your life. Choose God. Choose the cross and experience freedom.

Made in the USA
Columbia, SC
30 August 2018